TAPESTRY

Threads of Life Woven by The Master

Asher A. Chanan-Khan, MD

TAPESTRY

Threads of Life Woven by The Master

Asher A. Chanan-Khan, MD

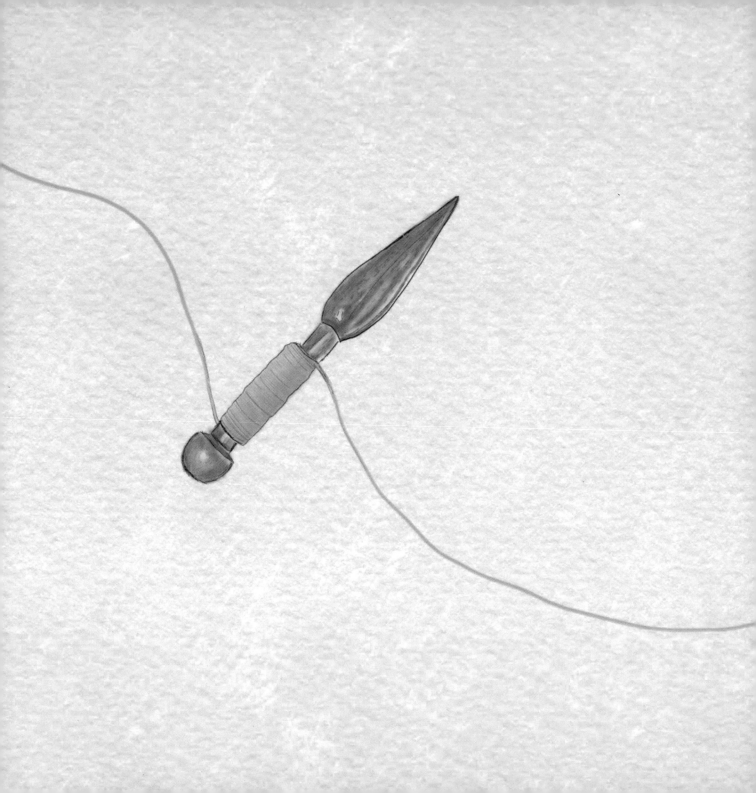

Tapestry

Asher A. Chanan-Khan, MD

Bridge-Logos

Newberry, FL 32669

Tapestry

Threads of Life Woven by The Master

Printed in India.

Library of Congress Catalog Card Number: 2022948047

International Standard Book Number: 9781-61036-290-0

Interior Design & Cover Design: Becky Patterson

Illustration: Samantha Nelson with Sam Nelson Art

This reflection is dedicated to

my son Matthew

Preface

The Lord fills our lives with extraordinary gifts of wonder and joy. In the midst of this life journey also come many challenges destined to trouble our souls. These often bring us to a standstill in the mud of sorrow. While the momentum of life helps us drag ourselves out of these sticky situations, some muddy stains remain permanently etched on the softness of our souls. With the joys of our lives, these unwanted tours of pain are also essential to complete our life's journey.

The construct of my life is no different than yours. My life, like yours, has had many joyful moments. These moments, every now and then, got overshadowed by gloomy mishaps that I would rather not want to have included in my life. Whenever I was in those more challenging times I could only look up and question my Lord "why" and plead for relief. Among the toughest of these was the loss of my son Noah and a bitter end to a happy, married life with a woman I could never stop loving. And I often found my heart wholly perplexed and in disarray as to how my life drifted so far away from the pattern of life I had designed in my mind. My final thread perhaps is wrapped around the terminal cancer diagnosis – the same disease I have dedicated my life as a physician to fighting.

Tapestry is a narrative of the dialogue that I found myself having with my Lord in those moments when I first learned of the terminal nature of my disease. This conversation with the Lord eased my soul and gave me all the answers to the many questions I had posed before Him over the years. Through this encounter, I witnessed my entire life – in His presence and through His perspective. He assured me that all the "good" and the "bad"– represented as the bright and dark threads – were essential to complete my life's tapestry perfectly. I learned that my life's vibrant-colored threads lean so much on the dull and dark ones. I realized that the Great Master knew precisely when and where to use which colors to make my life spectacular.

Our lives are God's masterpieces. Not one is frivolously or inconsiderately conceived. Each event, each incident, each laugh, and every single tear is measured and diligently weaved into our lives as perfect knots tying our whole life's story together. Once we know this, we can in faith believe that for all these knots that the Lord's hand ties, His heart is constantly yearning for and loving us. The darker times in our lives are not a reflection of His insensitivity or tactlessness but, in fact, a reminder of a greater love for us. He intentionally weaves our lives through these moments so we might be able to appreciate His amazing bounty awaiting us.

I hope reading *Tapestry* will allow you to relive many moments of similar importance in your life. I randomly touched a few threads in my life in this book, and I ask you to come before His presence and allow yourself to randomly touch a few threads from your life's tapestry as He continues to work on your story.

With Love,

Asher

The Master spoke yet
again. Tenderly He smiled
and said, "It's time, Son."
I looked up at Him.

"Time to come home, son."

I left my tools and smilingly
said, "Master, I am ready."

The Master spoke again,

"Yes, I know."

I asked, "What do you
have here, Master?"

"The tapestry I weaved for your life- It is almost done, son," replied the Master.

"How is it looking? May I please see it?" requested I.

"Yes, you may," said the Master. "

"Sometimes I let my people see their

tapestry before it is actually done."

I walked over to my Master as He gently upturned His handiwork and revealed the amazing vibrancy of my life's tapestry.

"Was my life this beautiful?" I asked.

The Master smiled and nodded, "Yes."

"It was a perfect life. Just the way I designed on this tapestry, one knot at a time. Not a thread fell out of its place," He said.

"I love the bright, vibrant colors,"
said I to the Master. "Is that how
you planned my life?"

The Master smiled contently. "I, too, like your bright and vibrant colors. I chose each of these colors especially for you, my son."

He then took my one hand, and gently placed it on the brightest weave in the tapestry....

Suddenly, my heart filled with joy.
A blissful smile embraced my lips
and my soul soared up as if floating
in the coolness of a gently breezed
blue summer sky... I remembered.

I remembered that time. It was the time
I first saw my son born, holding him,
smelling him, hugging him...

My whole world had stopped to
savor that moment then...

and yet again, it stopped as
my fingers slowly traced those
threads, reliving moments of joy.

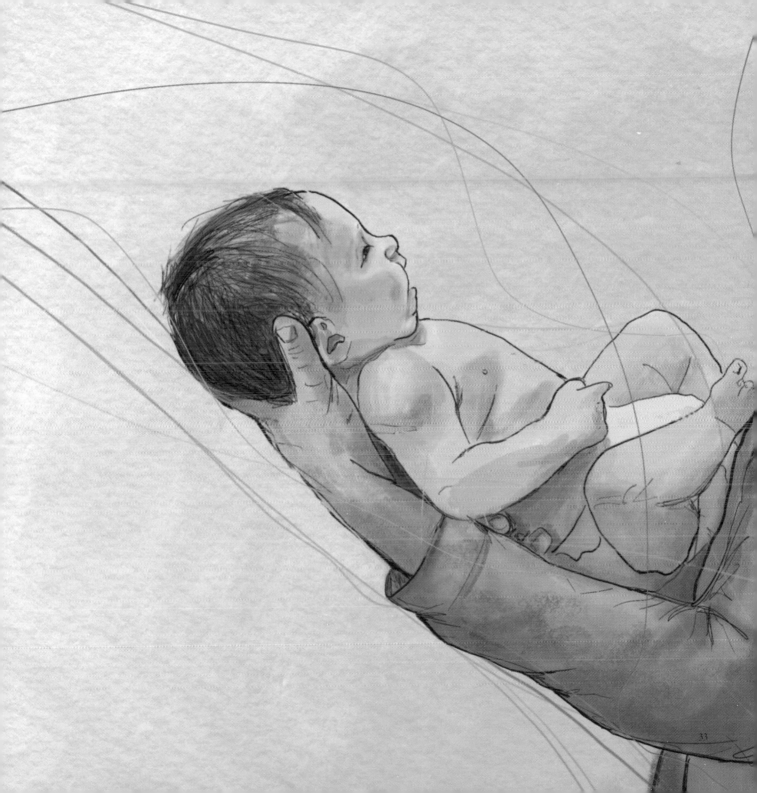

Gently I closed my eyes to stay there
a bit longer, encouraged by the
Master's soothing smile.

His fingers still rested on mine as
I sapped, once again, the joys of
those tender moments in my life.

My fingers eager to touch a few
other threads. The Master saw
that. He let me explore some more.

Gingerly, as my fingers randomly searched,
my heart started to trot anxiously, eager
of what else I may be able to unveil...

My fingers drifted towards a subdued,
black thread running beside the vibrant
flower I just touched. Should I touch?
Would I dare?

I saw the Master's smile fade just a little. His eyes tenderly touching my face with love, almost questioning if I really wanted to feel that color?

A tear rolled down my cheek...
I was already there!

The room seemed cold, a solitary
shiver plagued my spine, my senses
a bit muddled, as my heart sank and
my eyes could no longer hold the
weight of tears.

It's Christmas Eve and I hold, in my hands, the tiny body of my dead son. Standing over the frozen grave, I hear my bones crackle from the perpetual gray frost, my wife broken, tearless wailing in a surly silence of a frigid graveyard. A beginning of a long winter...

Was I strong or had weakness numbed me? Will I ever forget? Life came to an end then. There was no sun. There were no songs.

Amid the cold, icy, aimless wind that
breezed over the listless white snow,
wrapped a few uninteresting people
around a tiny grave. My world was
so dark, and then I saw it went even
darker. My fingers froze, and would
not want to leave.

Can I touch him one more time?

The rhythm of my heart struggled to pace. With each beat my heart felt once again a familiar throb that had secretly inflicted me for years.

My eyes finally found the Master
and He knew the answer.

Said He, "I needed a darker thread
to make the vibrant flower 'pop'
out better."

Softly, He took my hand in His, kissed my fingers, and spoke, "It is for your life's tapestry."

The Master continued to search me as
I stood wondering whether I wanted to
come back to the tapestry.

From the distance the tapestry was exquisite... the colors amazing, the patterns complex yet so complete, the knots so masterfully and skillfully placed... nothing amiss.

Composing myself, I dared again.
Some playful run of thread caught my
eyes. Eager was I to visit with them.

From the corner of my eyes I searched the Master. His face brightened again, nudging my pacing heart to expose the secret of those alluring colors tantalizing my curiosity.

Eagerly I broke loose from the captivity of my hesitation. Immediately happiness and joy filled me again.

I heard songs of delight, untamed boldness of my spontaneous laughter, and the exciting thrill of slowly unfolding mysteries of an untold life ahead. It was my wedding day.

How imperfectly complete that day was, how wonderfully designed those moments became, how amazing the promises of hope it brought. Many faces, many flavors, many prospects started to dance vividly before my eyes, all wrapped in an unceasing continuum of that day's merriment.

Yet my impassioned eyes remained
focused on the one that God sent to
walk beside me on this earth.

But this part of the tapestry was
surrounded by the darkest shroud,
a lost lotus drifting away aimlessly in
the bleakest of the ponds.

I did not need to look at the Master, I knew what lay hidden beneath these threads of my tapestry. I knew the familiar darkness of this shroud, for it still surrounded my soul and toiled upon my heart.

I need not touch these threads to
fathom the horridness they conceal.

Conniving faces of the cunning
litigators, the pangs of betrayal,
the despair of the lost paradise,
my fractured home, the scattered
splinters of her sacred vows. I
searched my heart only, and
not the threads of the tapestry.

Noticed I, the fervent hands of
the Master were back tying knots
into my tapestry.

I saw the Master pulling in the colors
of the rainbow into the threads that
flowed through His skilled fingers
pouring into my tapestry.

The Master focused, an intent frown
on His forehead as His fingers tying
and weaving together the knots that
will conclude the end of my tapestry.
Curious and unable to see, I
wondered about my son.

What color thread the Master will use,
to show the intense longing I felt in
watching him grow, the conversations
that I will miss, the affections I so am
accustomed to...?

The love that flows and binds us every day on this earth, the promises of this life that I so much wanted to watch unfold, the joys of unveiling the time-old mysteries of this world...yet once again by a new soul.

I wondered, what color had He
picked for the dreadful, untimely,
and inconvenient malady that
brandishes its ugly powers to
deport me from these simple
joys of an ailing father?

As the Master's fingers settled down
for the final few knots, His smile
invited me back to the tapestry.

My final wonders as He handed me

my life's tapestry to take a final look.

His eyes gleamed with joy, His hands cheerful and His face satisfied in the choices of the colors and patterns that He picked to weave in my tapestry.

Wondering if the last part of
my tapestry will be filled with
darker threads, I peered over
the Master's shoulder.

He knew my fear and

He put it to ease.

He gently directed my gaze towards
the brightest corner of His masterpiece,
filled with wild flowers, vibrant colors,
joyful overtones, playful vines that
seem to run endlessly in their own
exquisite delights.

A sense of thrill, a sense of
peace, a sense of happiness,
and a sense of gratification.
Pleasures abound, a blissful
soothing charm elated my soul.

There were no dark,
but all vibrant threads.

Puzzled I looked, why no reflections
of the work I leave undone, the things
unseen, the quests unfettered, the
love I still sought and the promises
yet to be fulfilled?

Master smiled and said, "It's your
faith, son. Faith always brings the
best colors out in the tapestry.
Your faith is completed today."
I nodded, and it all made sense.

He handed me my tapestry, and as
I glanced upon it one last time, I saw
no dark threads but only the beauty
of my Master's skill.

I loved my tapestry and
thanked my Master with
a single tear.

"I am ready, Master," said I.

"I know," said the Master.

About the Author

Asher A. Chanan-Khan, M.B.B.S., MD, is a leading cancer researcher and a cancer clinician. Blending medical education, research, and patient care, Asher is a Professor of Medicine and Oncology at Mayo Clinic in Jacksonville, Florida. His cancer research laboratory discovers and develops new cancer drugs to heal patients with blood cancers. He is actively engaged in training the next generation of cancer physicians and researchers as he mentors a select few. He is highly sought after as a contributor of insight and expertise for cancer clinical trials and as a collaborator on new discoveries.

Asher spent the first twenty years of his life in Pakistan before moving to the very heart of the US: New York City. He completed his medical training in NYC, with an internship and residency from the College of Physicians & Surgeons at Columbia University and then a Fellowship in Oncology & Hematology from New York University. In the year 2000 he joined the country's first Comprehensive Cancer Center, Roswell Park Cancer Institute in Buffalo, where he practiced before coming to the Mayo Clinic in Jacksonville, Florida, in 2011.

Asher is a vibrant part of the Jacksonville community, demonstrating his appreciation for art, music, animals, church, and French cuisine. He serves in many volunteer, philanthropic capacities, including an international organization committed to relief efforts for bonded slaves in Southeast Asia. Asher shares thought-provoking stories of life as a religious minority - growing up as a Christ-follower in a predominantly Muslim country. He also enjoys sharing his humorous adventures as a novice immigrant in the United States.

Despite all of the professional and personal accolades, Asher considers his son Matthew to be the most vibrant thread in his life—the biggest blessing and gift from the Lord. Soccer tournaments, chocolate eclairs, kitchen counter science experiments, worship music, and jam sessions are facets of the father-son relationship that delight all who are privileged to get a glimpse of their affection and devotion. And not to be forgotten is another thread -- that of their English Springer Spaniel named Adonis, who tags along almost everywhere.

All proceeds from the sale of this book are donated to support the education and freedom of Christian bonded slaves in Southeast Asia. Open Hands Global USA is a 501(c)3 Non-Profit Organization. To learn more please visit www.openhandsglobal.com or @openhandsglobal (Twitter, Instagram, Facebook).

Asher's previous book, *Lazarus & Me: Living Life in Lazarus Moments*, is available on Amazon and Barnes & Noble. In this book, Asher journeys with the reader through his first bout with cancer which coincided with his pinnacle of discovery of cancer treatments as a leading cancer researcher and clinical oncologist.

Asher can be reached at www.chanankhan.com